1 in 4:

Life After Loss

Tomeekè R. Hayes

Scripture quotations are taken from the Holy Bible, New Living Translation, copyright © 1996, 2004, 2015 by Tyndale House Foundation. Used by permission of Tyndale House Publishers, Inc., Carol Stream, Illinois 60188. All rights reserved.

ISBN: 979-8-218-82211-8

To Gerald and Sia, the only two people who know how my heartbeat feels from the inside. You are my reason, my inspiration, and my greatest joy. God made no mistakes when He chose you to be my children. My prayer for you both is that you always stay true to yourselves and pursue what you are passionate about. You bring light and love into my life, and for that, I am eternally grateful. May your paths be filled with wonder and your hearts with courage.
Love, Mommy

"In the depths of grief, we find the seeds of resilience. Through the shadows of loss, we learn the power of hope and the strength within to embrace life anew."
TOMEEKÈ R. HAYES

Contents

Introduction

In the tapestry of life's journey, some moments weave themselves into our very being, shaping who we are and how we see the world. This story, 1 in 4: Life After Loss, was born from one such moment—a personal narrative that delves into the profound and often silent experience of miscarriage.

Miscarriage affects approximately one in four pregnancies, yet it remains a topic shrouded in silence and stigma. By sharing my own story of loss and the transformative lessons that emerged from this deeply personal tragedy, I hope to break that silence.

The title, 1 in 4, reflects a stark reality—one in four pregnancies end in miscarriage. It is a statistic that is both sobering and isolating, yet it also connects a vast community of individuals who have endured this silent heartache. Through my story, I aim to shed light on the often-hidden struggles faced by many, breaking the silence and building a bridge of understanding and compassion.

Writing this story has been a journey of reflection and healing. By sharing my experience, others who have walked a similar path will find solace in knowing they are not alone.

Exploring the Chapters

Each chapter of this book represents a significant stage in my journey:

Life Changes: Here, we explore the initial joy and anticipation of new life, a time filled with dreams and aspirations for the future.

Loss of Life: This chapter delves into the many phases of my miscarriage and the profound emotional rollercoaster that followed my loss.

Rebirth: After a loss, there is a need to rediscover oneself and redefine life's purpose. This chapter captures the essence of starting anew amidst the ashes of grief.

Life Lessons: Finally, this chapter shares the invaluable lessons I learned. Healing is a multifaceted process, and this chapter offers insights into the emotional, physical, and spiritual recovery that followed my miscarriage.

Through these pages, I hope to offer a narrative that is both intimate and universal, empowering others to find their own strength and voice after loss. My story serves as a testament to the resilience of the human spirit and the possibility of finding beauty and purpose in the wake of tragedy.

As you read, I invite you to embark on this journey with me. Together, let us embrace the power of shared stories and the healing that comes from connection and understanding. In the face of loss, there is a way forward, and through my story, I hope to illuminate that path for myself and others.

Life Changes

It is said that the moment you find out that you are pregnant, your whole life changes. Well, what if you find out that you are pregnant and that you may have miscarried within the same appointment? This is where my story begins. I soon realized that I am 1 in 4.

New Life

Around February 3, 2016, I was scheduled to see the doctor to confirm whether I was pregnant. While driving to the clinic, I was full of mixed emotions because I was not sure if I was pregnant or starting menopause. I was 36 years old at the time, and my cycles had begun to shorten and become irregular.

Upon arrival, I signed in and had a brief wait before the nurse called me back to the exam room. After going back to see the nurse, I gave a urine sample and anxiously awaited the results. Shortly thereafter, I heard the words I had hoped to hear: "Congratulations, you are pregnant." I was thrilled to hear that I would be assisting God with the miracle of bringing another child into the world.

Next, the nurse began to prep my belly for an ultrasound to determine how far along I might be. While the nurse was performing the ultrasound, I could tell that something was off. That room was utterly silent, and the nurse looked concerned. I struggled with saying anything out of fear that the nurse might tell me that something was wrong. I finally got the courage to ask a question. I asked, "Is everything ok"? I knew that everything was not ok, but I could not think of another question to ask. The nurse stammered but told me that things were fine, but I knew she was not being candid.

A few minutes passed by as the nurse continued to take measurements of my belly, and then she finally told me the truth. There was no heartbeat. Based on my measurements, the nurse estimated that I was around 6 to 8 weeks pregnant. However, due to the absence of a heartbeat, a transvaginal ultrasound was performed to determine the actual size of the fetus. This ultrasound indicated that, based on the size of the fetus, I was only about 4 weeks pregnant, at most. The nurse instructed me to follow up with my regular doctor and reassured me that everything was ok. She believed that since I was only 4 weeks pregnant, I would hear a heartbeat soon. The nurse told me not to worry and sent me home with a beautiful pastel-colored crochet hat. I felt in my heart that I was pregnant with a little girl, and that hat served as confirmation for me. So, I still had hope and placed my faith in God.

I tell you, you can pray for anything, and if you believe that you have received it, it will be yours. ~ Mark 11:24

I believed that if I prayed fervently, everything would work out fine. I prayed that by my next appointment, I would hear a heartbeat. I remember telling my partner the details of the appointment, and he did not appear fazed at all by what I said. Looking back, this moment was an indication of what was meant to come, but I brushed it off and continued to pray.

Still No Heartbeat

A few weeks passed by, and my belly kept growing, but still there was no heartbeat. After a follow-up appointment with the doctor, I was still being told not to worry, it was still early. It was possible that I would hear a heartbeat any day now.

Now pause for a moment. Can you imagine the amount of stress and anxiety that I was experiencing during this time? My emotions swung like a pendulum, back and forth from joy and excitement to sadness and grief constantly. I only told two people besides the father that I was pregnant. Although I wanted to discuss how I was feeling with someone, I thought that I could not share my feelings with anyone. I did not believe that they could comfort me. I assumed that neither of the three people could say anything to make me feel better or calm my anxiety.

So, during this time, I isolated myself and cried a lot. Most days, I could not even focus on anything but my prayers for a viable pregnancy. But as we know, life does not stop for anyone. I had to keep swimming.

The Florida Bar Exam

So, I forgot to mention. While these doctor visits were going on, I was studying for the bar exam. Yep! You heard that correctly. I was studying day and night for the bar exam and working at a law firm part-time. My prayer every day was that my baby would be ok. I remember specifically asking God to save my baby. I now believe that deep down inside, I started to lose hope in what the doctors were saying, but my faith would not allow me to give up on God.

I sat for the bar exam on February 23- 24, 2016. For two days, I prayed that my baby would live. Although I cannot tell you what subjects or material were presented on the bar exam, I completed each section of the exam, on both days. I even socialized with other exam takers, but inside, I was crumbling.

I received my bar exam results on April 11, 2016; I failed the bar exam. Oddly, I was not that upset about failing the bar exam because I knew that I could retake the exam. What I feared most was losing my baby and that fear was slowly becoming a reality.

> *For I know the plans I have for you," says the Lord.*
> *"They are plans for good and not for disaster, to*
> *give you a future and a hope. ~ Jeremiah 29:11*

This is one of the scriptures that I held on to. I repeated it back to God daily because His word shall not return void.

Loss of Life

*Four days later, on Friday, April 15, 2016, I drove myself
to the emergency room due to excessive bleeding and severe
abdominal pain. I remember pulling up to the hospital valet in
so much pain that I could barely walk. Looking back, I know it
was only the grace of God that got me to the hospital safely.*

My Miscarriage

Sometime in March 2016, the doctors finally concluded that I did not have a viable pregnancy, and I experienced a miscarriage. My body still behaved as if I had a viable pregnancy, and my belly kept growing, but I likely miscarried around six weeks.

Initially, the doctors believed that my body would naturally recognize the loss and pass the pregnancy tissue. I was told that this was the safest route and that it was common for some miscarriages to take longer to complete. However, my body never recognized the loss, and my belly continued to grow.

The doctors finally prescribed medicine to assist my body in passing the pregnancy tissue. Sadly, I experienced uncommon vaginal bleeding from the prescribed medicine. I could barely walk, and I was soaking, pad after pad. I discussed going to the ER with my partner. As we prepared to leave the house, he noticed some blood had dripped on the bathroom floor and the toilet. Although I was visibly in pain, his concern regarding cleaning up the blood spots overshadowed my need for medical care. I clearly remember that he started to fuss about the blood and began to clean the bathroom. I thought that it was very possible that I could die that day, so I grabbed my keys and drove myself to the hospital.

Bless those who curse you. Pray for those who hurt you. ~Luke 6:28

The hospital was 9 miles away. According to the GPS, it should take 17 minutes to get to the hospital from my house, but I do not remember anything about the drive there. I only remember arriving at Winnie Palmer Hospital and passing my keys to the valet. My partner arrived shortly after me.

Emergency Surgery

The triage nurse asked me the standard laundry list of questions and asked for my pain level on a scale of 1 to 10. I told the nurse that my pain level was at 10. The nurse looked confused and instructed me to have a seat in the waiting room; someone would be with me shortly. I walked out of the small office and made my way toward the chair in the waiting room. Suddenly, things began to look dim, as if a dark veil had been pulled over my eyes. I told my partner that I felt like I would faint. My partner called for a nurse and told the nurse how I was feeling. A few moments later, before the nurse could get a wheelchair, I fainted in the waiting room.

When I came to, the room looked dark, and I could not see very well. I heard the staff talking, but I could not make out everything that was said but, I knew they said, we need to stop the bleeding. The nurses finally took me to a room for an examination.

While lying in the exam bed, my sheets had to be changed a couple of times due to the blood loss. I had conversations with the nurse about random subjects while awaiting the doctor's arrival. One thing that stuck out to me was the nurse said, I did not appear to be in that much pain because I was talking. That statement was odd to me because even though I was visibly weak and bleeding out on the floor a few moments earlier, my pain levels still appeared to be in question. I told this nurse, just like I told the first nurse, my pain level was a 10.

Eventually, a doctor arrived and completed an examination. They tried everything to stop the bleeding. At one point, the doctor was continually pressing down on my stomach to pass the tissue, which helped but, the bleeding would not stop. The doctor deduced that some pregnancy tissue remained in my body and I would need to have a D&C, which stands for dilation and curettage. D&C is a procedure in which the cervix is dilated, and the lining of the uterus is surgically scraped. The doctor believed that a D&C was the only option left to stop the bleeding at this point.

Since the doctor ordered a D&C, we were told that I would be staying in the hospital, at least overnight. So, my partner left to get an overnight bag and take care of some personal business. After my partner left, the staff asked if I would like to see the Chaplain for prayer, while I awaited an open operating room. I responded yes and waited for the Chaplain's arrival. As I waited for the Chaplain, I began to pray and sing gospel songs. How many of you know that sometimes, even when you are alone, you need to have praise and worship to shift the atmosphere?

> *God is our refuge and strength, always ready*
> *to help in times of trouble. ~ Psalm 46:1*

I decided that it was probably best if I called my family at this point. I called my mom and gave her a brief overview of why I was in the hospital and what was about to take place. I believed that should anything go wrong, it would be better if my family heard the story from me now rather than my partner after the fact.

When the Chaplain entered my room, I was smiling and talking to the nurse. The Chaplain also mentioned that I did not appear to be in pain. But this time, the sarcastic undertone was missing, and the Chaplain seemed relieved. The Chaplain told me that on his way to my room, God said to him that "the lady you are going to see, she knows my voice. You can talk to her."

After several minutes of small talk, the Chaplain asked if my partner would return soon, as the Chaplain was waiting for my partner to pray with us. I instructed the Chaplain to go ahead and pray. After the prayer, the Chaplain told me that God said, "I was walking through the valley of the shadow of death". That statement confirmed that I would live through this traumatic experience.

Even when I walk through the darkest valley, I will
not be afraid, for you are close beside me. Your rod and
your staff protect and comfort me. ~ Psalm 23:4

The Light

After the Chaplain left, I alerted the nurse that I had to use the restroom. The nurse asked me if I could walk. I responded, I think so and the nurse sent me down the hall to the restroom alone. I remember walking to the restroom and sitting down on the toilet. Everything after that was something out of a movie scene. I fainted again.

While unconscious, I saw a bright, yellowish light. The light was almost golden, like the sun, and it felt warm and comforting. I began to walk towards the light, where I had a delightful conversation with a man. I do not remember what we discussed or what the man looked like. I only remember how I felt. The conversation felt familiar, the man was no stranger, and I felt safe. When I was speaking with the man, I began to hear others calling my name repeatedly. I opened my eyes and saw that I was lying on the restroom floor, surrounded by medical staff, waving something under my nose.

The doctor asked me how I felt and what I remembered. I told him that I felt fine, and I remember walking to the restroom, and then I was talking to him. The doctor stated that I was not having a conversation with him at all. Later, the staff told me that at some point before fainting, I must have pulled the emergency cord by the toilet. I do not remember pulling the cord or falling to the ground. The nurse also told me that when the medical staff came into the restroom, my mouth was moving, but there was no sound coming from my mouth. Apparently, I was in this state for a few minutes, alarming the medical staff.

I got up off the floor, with help from the staff, and started talking as usual and smiling. Everyone looked perplexed, and the nurses were instructed not to allow me to walk off alone again. Shortly after returning to the exam room, a room in the surgical suite opened up. It was time to be taken upstairs for emergency surgery.

Rolling Veins

I have stretch marks on the inside of my arms and rolling veins. This makes it hard for some nurses to draw blood or start IVs. On this night, the nurse tried multiple times to start the IVs to prep for surgery, but she could not get a "good vein." Eventually, the nurses called an IV Tech to finish the job.

While awaiting the IV Tech's arrival, I recall telling the nurses, who would accompany me into surgery, that I would not require surgery. I told them that the bleeding would stop on its own. One of the nurses, who had prayed with me, said "I pray that you do not need surgery, but we are here just in case."

The IV Tech arrived shortly after with a small ultrasound machine. The machine located a "good vein," and the anesthesiologist awaited final authorization from the doctor to move forward. When the doctor came back into the room to examine me, the bleeding had stopped, and the doctor said that surgery was no longer required. By this time, my partner had returned to the hospital with clean clothes and homemade food, rich in iron.

So be strong and courageous! Do not be afraid and

do not panic before them. For the Lord your God
will personally go ahead of you. He will neither fail
you nor abandon you. ~ Deuteronomy 31:6

Although surgery was no longer required, I lost a lot of blood. My hemoglobin levels were critically low, so a blood transfusion was necessary.

Contaminated Blood

I know that I said that all of this occurred in the year 2016, but I am old enough to remember the "Infected Blood Scandal" in the Eighties. Although I knew that science and technology had improved, the memories of people getting infected with diseases through transfusions were haunting me and with everything I had been through that day, reason was out the window. I almost started to believe the medical staff was intentionally trying to harm me. So, I initially refused the proposal for a blood transfusion. I asked the doctor if the transfusion was necessary because I did not want contaminated blood in my body.

The doctor explained the dangers of critically low hemoglobin levels, this was a life or death situation. The doctor went on to highlight the safety measures and precautions that are now taken with blood donation and preparation for use, but I was still hesitant. I asked for a moment to process what was going on. When the doctor left, I prayed and discussed the transfusion with my partner. Later, I agreed to the transfusion. I received two units of blood throughout the night and stayed overnight in the hospital.

I came home from the hospital the next day, Saturday, April 16, 2016. I consider this day my rebirth day. When I was released, I was in a weakened state, looking like a shell of myself, but I was alive to tell the story.

I will not die; instead, I will live to tell what the Lord has done. ~ Psalm 118:17

May 5, 2016

Rebirth

*I tried to focus on the positives, I AM ALIVE,
and I did not require surgery.*

Recovery

Soon after I arrived home that Saturday, my mom and my son were walking through the door. My mom drove down from Tallahassee, Florida, to "lay eyes on me." I do not know how much my son knew about the situation at the time, but he was happy to see his mom, and I was overjoyed to see him. That is all that mattered. In that moment, I was grateful that I was alive, and I could physically touch my living child.

The doctors told me that it would take time to recover. I understood that to mean that I was in for a lengthy process to recover both physically and mentally. I tried to focus on the positives, I AM ALIVE, and I did not require surgery. Seems simple, right? But oh no, it is the furthest thing from the truth.

In reality, my body had betrayed me. A woman's body is meant to carry children, right? So, why didn't my body perform as expected? Was I broken? Would I ever be able to have another child? These are the many questions that ran through my mind daily. Additionally, no one could ever prepare me for the amount of guilt I felt for losing my baby.

Yep! I blamed myself. I told myself that I did not pray enough. I did not eat the right food. I studied too much and stressed the baby. All the statements above were just the tip of the iceberg. Sadly, I even asked God why He was punishing me. I asked Him to reveal my sins that took my baby.

Now, there are a few things that I do not play about, the top things being my God and my Faith. So, you can imagine that I had become someone whom I did not recognize. For the first time in my life, I felt like maybe I had run out of grace and my sins had come back to consume me. I started repenting for things I did as a child. I repented for the lies that I told in high school. I was legit asking God to forgive me for lying to my parents in the 12th grade. That time when I said that I was at the library but I was at my boyfriend's house. I was lost, and I could not focus. However, I showed up every day for work and others, as if nothing ever happened. I smiled through the pain and tried to nurse myself back to health.

For years, I showed up for weddings, birthdays, baby showers, funerals, and heartbreaks. I poured into people while I cried myself to sleep every night. I pretended that I was not broken because I did not have time to break down. After all, no one was going to save me if I did. No one could understand what I was feeling, and I could not bear to hear anyone else tell me how strong I was.

At least that is what I thought because no one ever talks about pregnancy loss. There was no one sharing the story of their loss experience. I remember one of my friends sharing her journey through disappointment and loss many years ago, but she was the only person that I could recall being open about her experiences. Even my partner functioned as if things were back to normal. We did not talk about the miscarriage for years, and when I would bring the subject up, he would say, "I cannot talk about it", as if it were so easy for me to recount one of the most traumatic experiences of my life.

> *Weeping may last through the night, but joy comes in the morning. ~ Psalm 30:5*

Confessions

It took years for me to say the words, "I had a miscarriage". I did not have the language to describe the way I was feeling or the sadness of losing a child that I never actually got to meet. I felt lonely and isolated even when I was in a room full of people. I was wounded, and although I believed that I wanted to be better, there were some harsh truths that I would need to face.

Truth number one: I had to determine if this was the man that I wanted to spend the rest of my life with. Based on his behavior during my miscarriage and after. Did I trust him to be there for me mentally and physically? I believed that he saw me as some invincible robot because while at the hospital, he questioned my level of pain, too. According to the nurses and my partner, people in pain do not talk or smile. My partner believed that I confused the medical staff because I kept talking. I already blamed myself for my miscarriage and now I felt blamed for the poor level of care that I received from the hospital staff.

Truth number two: I had to reconcile how I would feel if I never conceived another child. Would I always feel like something was missing? I planned my entire life out in elementary school. I was supposed to have three children but here I was going on 37, mother of one, believing that my body might fail me again.

The journey to recovery was arduous, but reassessing my life was necessary to move into the next chapter of my life.

> *And you will know the truth, and the truth*
> *will set you free. ~ John 8:32*

Life Lessons

Trust God even when you cannot see God.

Healing

I am here to tell you that you can heal. In moments of doubt, lean into your faith and your support system. Your support system will lift you up and give you the strength to press on a little further.

Put your energy into healing mentally and physically. Focus on being the best version of yourself.

Do not focus on the when. The battle is won in small steps. Putting one foot in front of the other is your goal initially. The rest will come.

> *Wait patiently for the Lord. Be brave and courageous.*
> *Yes, wait patiently for the Lord. ~ Psalm 27:14*

Get into your Word and stay there until your breakthrough occurs.

I would love to tell you that one day you will wake up and everything will feel "normal" again. However, that would be a lie, and lies do not help anyone heal.

The truth is that day by day, the tears dry up. Then one day, you will look up and life will seem a little brighter.

God will heal your heart.

Trust God

The most important lesson that I learned throughout this process was that I can have all the plans in the world, but I must trust God that His plan is better. I made a lot of decisions based on what I thought was going to happen and what I thought should happen but, at the end of the day, the only thing that mattered was what God said.

> *For the Lord God is our sun and our shield. He gives us grace and glory. The Lord will withhold no good thing from those who do what is right. ~ Psalm 84:11*

When I was initially told that my pregnancy may not be viable, I said, "I know it is going to be ok because I trust God", but what I was saying was, I know that my baby is going to live because I trust God. What I learned was that although my baby did not live, I still must trust God. You see, God's plan is always greater than our own.

God sees what is going to happen 20, 30, or even 40-plus years down the road, while we are only looking at the next 24 to 48 hours. For all I know, there could have been all types of complications with this pregnancy or my baby. So, God said no, I am going to protect you from things that you cannot see.

Oftentimes, when we are going through our valley

experiences, we lose sight of the fact that God is still in control.

Trust in the Lord with all your heart;
do not depend on your own understanding. ~ Proverbs 3:5

We must always remember these basic facts:

1. When we do not get the outcome that we desire, God is still in control.

2. When we fast and we pray, and God does something contrary to what we prayed for, God is still in control.

3. Trust God in all things, through all things, and for all things.

4. God's plans are always greater than our own.

5. God knew what we would go through before we were even born.

6. God makes no mistakes.

God is the greatest, and through this situation, my faith grew stronger. My prayers went deeper, and I examined my life. God knew things that I did not know, and He still showed me grace and mercy along the way. This is evident because when I was stretched out on that hospital floor, talking to a man, walking towards the light, that could have been my last day on earth. However, God said no, you shall live.

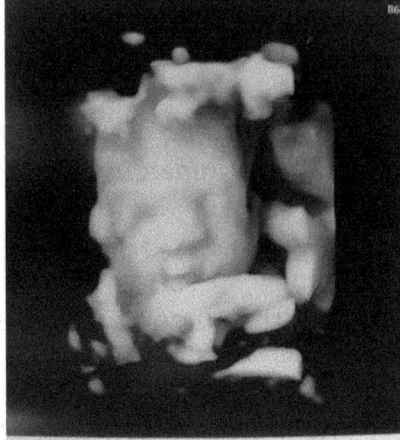

Because God is faithful, God gave me another beautiful baby. My rainbow baby was born one year and 4 months after my miscarriage. This time around, my pregnancy was smooth sailing. I was not sick, nor did I experience any complications. Now the labor, that is a different story, for another day.

My little rainbow baby was born on my oldest brother's birthday, weighing 6lbs 1oz—bright-eyed, happy, little peaceful Ava. In Hebrew, Ava means "life" or "to live". My daughter is proof that there is life after death.
While my pregnancy with my rainbow baby was healthy, in the back of my mind, I thought things could go wrong at any moment. I used to hold my breath at every appointment because I was afraid we would not hear her heartbeat. I was also overly cautious with everything. After each appointment, the excitement would return, but the nervousness would never completely go away.

I am so thankful that God spared my life and saw fit to breathe life into my womb again. You cannot tell me anything about the God that I serve because time and time again, God has shown me that He loves me and He is concerned with every detail regarding my life.

But those who trust in the Lord will find new strength. They will soar high on wings like eagles. They will run and not grow weary. They will walk and not be faint ~ Isaiah 40:31

About The Author

Tomeeké R. Hayes

Tomeeke' is a Christian, mother, life coach, professional, and eternal optimist who is passionate about empowering individuals to create the lives they truly desire. With a rich tapestry of experiences marked by transitions and transformations, Tomeeke' often found herself reflecting on the question, "What now?"

Tomeeke' embraces a renewed mindset and perspective on life. She believes that a new journey awaits each of us.

Books By This Author

Chrysalis Journal

Like the chrysalis stage in a butterfly's life, this journal encourages introspection and reflection, allowing users to delve deeply into their thoughts, emotions, and experiences. Through carefully crafted prompts and exercises, the journal facilitates a deeper understanding of one's true self, helping to unveil hidden potential and foster positive change. By committing to regular entries, users can track their progress, celebrate their achievements, and identify areas for further development. Ultimately, The Chrysalis Journal acts as a supportive companion, guiding individuals as they evolve into the best version of themselves.

www.ingramcontent.com/pod-product-compliance
Lightning Source LLC
Chambersburg PA
CBHW060548030426
42337CB00021B/4483